City of Stars

City of Stars

An anthology of love poems for Frankston

Edited by Avril Bradley

In honour of Nan McClelland (1879–1961)

City of Stars: an anthology of love poems for Frankston
ISBN 978 1 74027 991 8
Copyright © text individual contributors 2015
Cover photograph by Michelle Leber of *Poet's Desk*, sculpture by
David Murphy (part of Frankston Coastal Arts Trail)

First published 2015 by
GINNINDERRA PRESS
PO Box 3461 Port Adelaide 5015 Australia
www.ginninderrapress.com.au

Contents

Foreword		7
1 'the allegro of the scavenging eye'		**9**
Beginnings	Warrick Wynne	11
seven moments	Glenn Harper	12
The Flow of Things	Anne Elvey	13
This Place	Marjorie D. Ward	14
Frankston Train	Garth Madsen	15
An Urbane Affair	Rhonda Jankovic	16
Director's Cut	Mary Jones	17
Frankston Station	Gwen McCallum	18
Bayside suburban	Anne Elvey	19
Under Ti Tree	Marjorie D Ward	24
down Oliver's	Avril Bradley	25
2 'beauties of the centre court'		**27**
Safe Haven	Rhonda Jankovic	29
At Kananook Creek	Anne Elvey	30
The Fine Art of Surfacing	Michael Potter	31
Superwomen	Garth Madsen	32
Wind-borne	Avril Bradley	34
The Fairies and I	Nan McClelland	35
The Raspberry-Coloured Hand-knitted Cardigan in the Salvos at Frankston	Jennifer Compton	36
Afghan Restaurant	Mal Morgan	37
The Day it Snowed in Frankston	Warrick Wynne	38
Wells Street Updated	Avril Bradley	39
Wedding Train	Warrick Wynne	40

3 'a box of astronomical delights' — **41**

The Frankston Massage	Jennifer Compton	43
Antipodean Home	Ann Simic	45
An English immigrant's letter from Frankston	Avril Bradley	46
In the Littoral	Philton	47
Looking at Oliver's Hill in Autumn	Avril Bradley	49
The Pyramids	Garth Madsen	50
Tardis	Mary Jones	51
City of Stars	Gwen McCallum	52
The end of the world	John Bradley	53

Contributors — 54

Acknowledgements — 57

Foreword

The poet Nan McClelland is the inspiration for this collection of poetry. She is celebrated in David Murphy's *The Poet's Desk*, a sculpture I glimpse from my balcony amidst the dunes on Frankston beach. Nan hosted the first children's programme on ABC radio, inaugurated the Peninsula Arts Society(1954), drove an ambulance for Frankston Hospital, and bequeathed money to establish the McClelland Art Gallery and Sculpture park. With her brother Harry, she lived in an artistic enclave in Palm Court, Long Island, Frankston. Of the several original buildings, only the old barn remains as an historic marker and weathered defender of uncertain ground, amongst the contemporary structures surrounding it.

My thanks to all poets who submitted their work, the editors of Five Islands Press, Pulse Publications and the Trustees of the Estate of A.M. McClelland, who generously allowed the reprinting of some poems in the anthology, Michelle Leber whose photograph makes an elegant cover design, Garth Madsen, John Jenkins and John Bradley for invaluable help, Brenda and Stephen Matthews of Ginninderra Press. Brenda's delightful cards and letters kept me focused when panic struck and courage faltered.

I wish all readers joy in the play of shine and shade on the sea, and the rush of the streets, as they journey through these love poems for Frankston.

Avril Bradley

1

'the allegro of the scavenging eye'

Beginnings

He has returned at last to his origins,
still standing constructions
obscured now by less likely plantings,
his handiwork becoming dispensable.
Everything has grown since those days, he says,
reciting the names of the dead;
the great entertainers in the third house,
the fisherman whose boat never left the beach,
the woman with the breast removed;
not all growth is to be remarked upon, it seems.

He has returned to these beginnings,
though he must know the days of the beach sales,
a man in a dark suit walking the shoreline
offering blocks of land to family groups
for sixty quid, are gone.
And Harry, the entertainer,
who, if you'd been working in the garden
or around the house all day,
would call you in
for a cup of tea or beer,
is five years dead,
in the Diggers' Home in Frankston.

Warrick Wynne

seven moments

Frankston City, mid-2014

a slow saturation
grey opens a day
birds already know

   morning fog
   three blue
   umbrellas

       unseen in public
       his hands
       tour her curves

       through a window
       on a wall
       hangs a high hem

   changes along a street
   i haven't walked
   for weeks

under lifting grey
we discuss the psychology
of the Frankston line

   footballers leave
   the ground
   still present

Glenn Harper

The Flow of Things

The storm has gathered to my walk
a bottle ring and a jellyfish
the size of my head. Navy
ribbons thread its gel.

I find an oar, a used
condom, a toy helicopter,
an offcut of new wood,
an inflated rubber glove

and a ball of roots crusted
with sand. Further on a many-
branched limb is turned
to smoothness by the sea. A fresh

sun is out. Five
water bottles are jewels,
one half-full with
the colour of tea. From

a car park ticket
I scrape the sand
to read the flow of things:
Fitzroy Street St Kilda.

There's a new cliff
near the pier. I climb
to the café. A gull tastes
a wide-eyed blowfish.

Anne Elvey

This Place

'And true plain hearts do in the faces rest' – John Donne (1572–1631)

Simple in name yet rich in grace,
A mosaic of music, literature, song and dance,
A theatre, galleries, parks and romance.
Frankston has City Fathers, computers too
Busy with messages lost or saved
in draft, or merely just deliciously daft.

I must pack and take a train
where folk with splendid hearts may go.
I'll stroll the old and lovely pier
I'll hear the mermaid singing, and then
along the boardwalk, where ti trees face
the shining sea, those forever, ever, trees
will comfort me.

Marjorie D. Ward

Frankston Train

Armpit to armpit, everyone sweats in a different language here. A woman's voice calls out the name of each station as we arrive, another scratching in the race of life, she says Mordialloc as if there can be less dialloc. Four urban minimalists play euchre, I cannot see if their cards are real or not. The echo girl sits under the 'no feet on seats' sign, her foot on the seat, the angle showing the curve of her in-step better than high heels, she tells her mobile phone that she was named after a car number plate. The powdered aeroplane blonde with an imitation pearl necklace becomes a delta, people pushing past her on either side. A drunk shouts, 'Of course, I'm smart. I went to school, didn't I?' A father, a mother scold their son as if they are trying to make him smile for the camera. The lowrider with an earring drops a water bottle at a ninja bitch's feet, there is an empty McDonalds wrapper under her seat and a browning apple core. The rainmaker with crickets in his ears drums the seat between his legs. The bonsai brunette sheds her black cardigan and flicks her anklet at the far border of my vision and I ask myself where her story ends and mine begins.

Garth Madsen

An Urbane Affair

Waiting for the second city
train I saw you for a second
crowd   surges
signal   smiles
station   stops
coffee   shops
chatter   heaps
fingers   touch
& on our second cup of tea
we organised a second date.

Rhonda Jankovic

Director's Cut

They filmed a famous scene on Platform 1,
another with a horse and cart in Young Street,
the beach scene further down the coast
recorded in a filming of the filming.

This was after Fred retired from dancing,
before Anthony became Norman and began
on all that trouble with his mother.
Gregory had moved on from Ahab,
between the white whale and the mockingbird.
Ava was always and eternally Ava,
although she never actually said
the quote recorded in the *Herald Sun*.

Famous, the lot of them, even then,
but not too proud to sign an autograph
for all the patients gathered on the cliff top
from Frankston Orthopaedic Hospital.

Mary Jones

Frankston Station

The kiosk lady opens the shutters,
yellow light pops into morning air.

Red blue and gold towers
cigarettes line the wall,
death in a packet or in the pages
of the *Herald Sun*.

'7.05 stopping all stations'

Open doors like mothers' arms
embrace the multitude, massage and jiggle,
spit them out when done,
repeating mechanically through the day
into evening.

The shutters close,
birds fly over, screech of a seagull gliding home.
On the empty seafront the best show
goes unnoticed.

Gwen McCallum

Bayside suburban

1

Port Phillip rucks and tears in the wind
and where the creek joins the bay, the lace
is tattered marl. Wild gulls pick

the day undone. A line of bleach ruptures
the denim cloud. Homes are like shirts
tucked into pants worn high, their prose

concealed from the RENOVATOR'S DELIGHT.
In the fraying suburb salt claws at the eaves.
A possum drops into a chimney, scrapes

at the wall, thumps and thumps. Though
her will has a rhythm insufficient to survive,
when a rope's let down, she climbs.

2

Lives pass in days of thin tar,
poured in patches where Frankston meets
the fluids left behind. Nudged by a late

patrol, a pale body is saying NO.
Young Street is slate rewritten with old
meals the gulls enjoy and the refuse of blood

and wine, the suburb's flesh, the greasy joes.
The air is deep fried palm oil.
Vinegar and salt are the commuters' tread, in odd

time with the lights. Only the click click
is even and the fixed eyes. Traffic slows
at Bunjil's statue. There's a mess of gulls.

3

A soft yellow light traces the shore's
length. The wind pushes southward along
the beach. A dog romps and a woman

dressed in rough wool casts a line.
Banksias are sculpted against the sky;
multiple prints emboss the shore recalling

absences – a palimpsest at the water's edge.
A small cliff is formed by tides and marks
the singular landscape of this one hour.

Spaces show the rhythm of bare feet.
Each indentation is dark with shadow
that defines it for the eye. The lemon light is blue.

4

The wind has left its skin in the old gum –
its buckled clock melts on Dali's page.
Impromptu, the gusts arrive in rough time

and follow a score this species will not
track. To their metre, seagulls group
and scatter. With scant pattern for the eye

they rise over Nepean Highway, and fall
past the scrub to the beach. In white and grey,
and the tucked orange legs, they are dye

that stains the air with wind's shift and drill.
And time is each ragged interval of the day,
the bent hands, the flowing clock, the skin.

5

Fine sand has settled in drifts. The long
afternoon smears the sky with petalled sun.
Walkers choose paths over sediment packed

tight, shells pressed into gravelled footing.
Strewer of a communion march, the day
empties its apron of blossom. The sand is thin

and brittle as a wafer. The skin is the tongue
to which it clings. The sacrament is celebrated slow
with gulls like restive children. As the light

deepens, the allegro of the scavenging eye
discovers – the tide that arrives with
the bounding sea, the soul-fetching night.

Anne Elvey

Under Ti Tree

Others have their Camelot, but this I have truly got,
a secret place with hidden pond,
a family of ducks, the verge beyond;
a bush creek hiding, its soft water gliding,
to the charméd name of sweet Sweetwater.

From fishing village to people's city,
some declare that's more the pity,
perhaps they are unaware there is a street,
William by name, that will lead you
to where ti trees grow in twisted grace,
embraced by winds from another place,
stroked by the sun that makes dandelions
throw their bright yellow carpet of
summer glow, and wayward creepers green
are seen showing small flowers blood red,
to catch the eye and turn the head.

In William Street, at its very end, darkling trees
throw soft shadows soft on bitumen black
that once was just a sandy track.
Track's end will take you where ti trees grow
and the eye can scan the rising blue of sea
and sky breathe the air that journeyed
from the south to sweeten and refresh the mouth.
This my friend is the back way to
a hill called Oliver.

Marjorie D Ward

down Oliver's

after Kevin Gillam's poem '*from Freo*' chosen as feature poem for
Poetry in Film festival, November 2012

it's the sudden plunge. it's the
chameleon sea. it's the whizz
of wheels. it's the windows of view.
it's the sunday drivers. it's the gasp
of awe. it's the sky's slipping scaffold.
it's the brake lights red glare.
it's down through the windows of view
it's road block. it's queue.

it's the unstopping. it's the un-
ravelling traffic. it's the under-
standing. it's the overview. it's
architecture on sand. it's rush
hour unplanned. it's the whiff
of sea salt. it's the stopping.

Avril Bradley

2

'beauties of the centre court'

Safe Haven

∧
= Like =
= birds =
= off a =
= wire =
= we fly =
= beyond barbed wire =
= beyond guards and lawyers. =
= And start again to celebrate life's banquet =
= of family friends and domestic events beyond =
= the stifling walls of detention centres. =
= To start =
= renewed =
= revitalised =
= lives =

Rhonda Jankovic

At Kananook Creek

On the bridge again I fret
        at the algaed mats, the silt
                scattered

with cans. Head-on
a flight approaches
        the length of the creek.   Two
                white arrowheads

pass to my
left – so close
        I expect to hear
        the rush of air.

                Silence.   One

resolves
        into the curved, tucked neck
        of an egret. The mate

escapes   my view.

A hoarse call trails them, as they follow
        the bent
                water –

Anne Elvey

The Fine Art of Surfacing

There are days when Peter wills the fish not to bite.
Baited line, bated breath.
The tug on the line, the change of tide,
the mouthing, the teasing tug of slack water.
Grappa in Peter's thermos beckons.
Peter mumbles like a crazy man, like crazy man
to keep those who would be close to him at bay.
He turns and watches the white horses charge Kananook Creek.
Nat shouts, 'Peter! Watch me!' then he dives.
Nat is a cormorant; his head bobs up, he chitters and dives again.
He scours the mud and sand beneath the pier,
looking for sunglasses or sinkers
or wallets or knives
or mobile phones
or the bleached barbs from the tails of deceased stingrays.
He squid jigs his way past upturned supermarket trolleys,
then rises, spits water
…sees the glare of the sun on the guano which covers the roof of Daveys Hotel.
He reaches for the crucifix on the silver chain around his neck.

Michael Potter

Superwomen

On the way back
from the Heatherhill Road shops
with bread rolls and milk
I pause
at the Bruce Park tennis courts
and watch the women play,

these are not the teenage
beauties of the centre court,
they are the women
of my generation with chunky
hips, stretchmarks
and boobs starting to droop,

still
I look at them
with the same eyes
I wore when
I was seventeen,

their awkward grace,
their vulnerability
captured between Germaine Greer
and what their mothers told them
they have lived the lives
of superwomen,

a tennis ball
thuds the net
and I only stand
for another rally or two
just long enough
to let them know
I am still watching.

Garth Madsen

Wind-borne

tribute to Annie May (Nan) McClelland (1879–1961)

When sea breezes seized the grass
all sounds floated atonal music
she was there above the sea's cymbal clash

gathering grasses, weaving words
into the fabric of her studio,
amongst dolls, dried flowers and birds.

Her parrot flew through the fairy bower
rested shoulder high on poetry
read in the children's radio hour.

'The Poet's Desk' plays the sea's eternal tunes
while sculptured ink and wine bottles spill
her memory wind-shuffling across the dunes.

Her spirit and the barn, still withstand
buffeting time, windblown seas and sand.

Avril Bradley

The Fairies and I

Some fairies gathered an armful of clover
and taking a spool of life's spinning wheel
Carded the wool
They picked from the dawn, sunrise and sunset
Long threads of gold

They picked from the sky a stout thread of blue
From the rainbow they picked every conceivable hue
They gathered from flowers, bees wing and the sea
They gathered from butterfly, moth and the bee
From moss stick and stone from pink and white clover.

They laughed in their glee as new hues discover
They never missed one shade
They wove good and true
Now who was this robe for?
Well who – I
Just look in the mirror and it will tell you.

Nan McClelland

From *The Poems and Works of Miss Nan McCLelland (1909–1959),* published by the Trustees of the Estate of A.M. McClelland Langwarrin c. 1990

The Raspberry-Coloured Hand-knitted Cardigan in the Salvos at Frankston

For a quick ecstatic moment I think – *Herdwick double knit!*
Just what I need to unravel and reknit for the poet's jumper.

And then my fingers know it for a triple and it is not Herdwick.
But still. I rethink my project, my brain goes click click click.

It is knit deliciously wrong side out with a cool curving basque.
The buttons are a wry comment on the high concept of 'cardigan'

It's a piece of work. But it is so small, who could it possibly fit?
Not her it was knitted for, over slow ticking hours, it is pristine.

Fallen fresh from the needles of a woman who can really knit.
It would be a sin to undo her gift. It would be mortally wrong.

Wool remembers what it was and would resist such declension.
Such consummate sewing up of it, such a smooth, even tension.

If it is still hanging on the rack on Tuesday when I go back,
I will buy it for eight bucks, salvage the buttons and unpick.

Jennifer Compton

Afghan Restaurant

Frankston

Tambur the long-necked lute
tabla the drums
   and a canary singing
in a bamboo cage   hung from the ceiling.
One of the finches bred for the cage
and off the streets   with their gangs
of Indian minahs   and soft footed felines.
But my day's a black dog   I hear very little.
I know no Afghani to speak to the waiter.
I look at the woman I love   who asks me
not to look tonight.
          I have no language
to respond   except the ubiquitous why?
I divide my korma   eat lamb with bread and rice
think of a butcher with his knife   a baker
with his yeast   but my butcher wants something
to make him rise   and my baker longs
to cut something fleshy   something red
and a philosopher wants to change his stone
for a geode   with the purest crystals inside.
Tonight I'll drink red wine   take a drug
for chronic pain   swallow hard   go into the
garden   sway with the rain and the crippled
moon   dance and dervish to tabla and tambur.
I'll learn Esperanto to commune with waiters
canaries and crows
          and the ones I love.
I'll start tomorrow.

Mal Morgan

The Day it Snowed in Frankston

for Eloise

The day it snowed in Frankston
the bay bit blue cold round the pier
and the joints ached and
the blue-white mussels broke sharp open as in a dream.
The day it snowed in Frankston
the creek came to a frozen halt
and the hire-boat engines grew heavy
with thick cold oil and stopped too.
The day it snowed in Frankston
that hour, that winter minute,
the highway slowed and stood still a moment
and a lady admiring the beauty slipped and fell.
The day it snowed in Frankston
the shopkeepers talked to customers hoarding in
and cramming and craning at the sky, 'it's just sleet',
'nah, that snow, mate', forgetting for a moment shoplifters
    and sales.
The day it snowed in Frankston
Eloise, aged six and curious, scooped up the scattered slush
from the gutter and placed it lovingly, mercifully
into the frozen incubator where it became, nothing.
She never forgot it.

Warrick Wynne

Wells Street Updated

Where the butcher, charity shops and a car park
have made way for a neon lit cinema, multicultural
eateries, a coffee barista, more charity and more
car parking.
Where only the rooftop seagulls add seaside flavour.
Where the corner pub spills its drunks into
Friday night palaver.
Where modern Montagues and Capulets wage
gang warfare from bikes and cars and later
fist out their animosities on the plaza.
Where on Thursdays the Farmer's Market closes
the street to angry motorists.
Where, toward the beach, cranes scrape
lifting eyes skyward to
new commercial heights.
Where community means the polite, young policeman
chatting to druggies whom he later apprehends for dealing.
Where in daytime a constant scribble of people sprawl
around the margins of a crossing, stopping traffic.
Where on winter Sunday nights wind from the station
howls down the emptiness to the sea.
Where anyone running has stolen something, anyone sleeping
is drunk, anyone standing still is a visitor and anyone almost
undressed is off for a grand night out!

Avril Bradley

Wedding Train

Reading the suburban narrative of the Frankston line
I ride the rise and fall of social class
rattling station to station, fault-lines
fraying along the bay's edge,
thinking of Larkin's wedding train,
the idea of brides, and grooms;
that we could even agree on such things any more.

Broken bricks, the backs of houses
grey sky bundled in unwinding backyards
bric-a-brac is too formal for this disassembly,
the flailing blue vinyl of the disposable pool
the swing-set and the ancient paling fences
blurring behind peppercorns.

We stop at an empty platform.
I don't expect any girl in a fine white dress
to climb aboard any time soon.

Warrick Wynne

3

'a box of astronomical delights'

The Frankston Massage

I ring at random and find a clinic opposite the Frankston Cemetery
and book an hour of someone touching me and letting my mind go.

He is a cheerful Aussie larrikin, he may have had a long liquid lunch.
He offers me a used towel, moist to the touch. I say I like to take my

underwear off. I'm taller than him by not much. We are of an age.
Where is the whale music, the feng shui bamboo, and the scented oil?

I lay myself down, naked under a clammy towel, prepared to give him
the benefit of the doubt. He won't shut up. His holiday in Norfolk Island

exercises him very much. Yap yap yap. As he storms my body, and yet
he finds the place in my shoulders from which all my unshed grief hangs.

Kudos for that. But he won't shut his trap. As he flips me back to front,
making eye contact. This is a bloody shambles, one of us has to get a grip.
I ask in a small voice, staring at the grimy ceiling, picking up the scent of
socks, if he does maybe many footballers? *Yeah, in February* – he replies.

When they begin training and start to feel it but not as much as I
   would
have hoped. He has hoped, as I have hoped, and we have come
   to this.

Neither of us is getting what we want. He wants to split my mind
   off from
my body's machine and pounce like a predator on all my hurts,
   I want

to be taken apart and tenderly caressed and then put back
   together again.
And now he wants his score, he gives himself a modest seven
   out of ten.

Out of the goodness of my heart I give him eight and a half,
   for trying,
for misunderstanding me so well. Tenderness for these peers of
   mine is

my downfall. His brothers have, with that same blithe
   myopic stare,
used me as clumsily and depended on my charity so many
   times before.

I walk back to Frankston all swinging shoulders like a front
   row forward
but my mind is graunching away out of kilter, out
   of whack.

Jennifer Compton

Antipodean Home

Much have I travelled through this spinning sphere
and seen the shores of many a foreign land
around the antipodes both far and near
I've laid me down and watched the sands
of time sift through the strands of all my life.

Now on the shores of Frankston I've washed up
another bit of wide-eyed flotsam here
seeing all the seasons' sights erupt
year after year, year after year
and hold me in their thrall.

The bush that backs upon our humble home
whispers its history in my eager ears
and tells me of the Bunurong who used to roam
now gone, fomenting guilt and fears:
they stepped so softly on the sandy loam.

Meandering through the pathways to the songs
of birds with colours that can sway the heart,
seeking to right the passage of our wrongs
redeem and expiate our part
and turn our trespass round.

Ann Simic

An English immigrant's letter from Frankston

Picture a seaside town in your head   then
subtract the ice-cream parlours, arcades, promenades
packed with sightseers, beer taverns, the big wheel
tired terraces offering B&Bs
spruikers proffering glamour and striptease.
Here only a few houses lob along for the private view.

Add a summer sky, blue, beyond believable
the sea itself magnet for daring deeds
acrobatic kite surfers, fishing tinnies, kayaks
jet skis, yachts, fragments blown about with
an occasional incident from a wooden pier,
a wide-toothed comb parting the waves.

Multiply the gulls scavenging by sea and shore.
Divide the population by four.

Avril Bradley

In the Littoral

We three step onto the beach
as others depart.
The first raindrops tell us why.
We keep walking
umbrellas our one concession.

We chat towards the pier
a jutting magnet
drawing our feet to its planks.
Rain-marbled waves
chop around us.
Beyond the drops
pink tips speculate
a sunset.

At jetty's end
our bright brollies are
beacons in the turbulence,
a signal for would-be intrepids;
the boy who wheelies with
his bike inches from the edge,
the power-walking duo who
up their strut when we look
and the old lady who chides us
for having umbrellas
(yet happy to accept cover under mine).
Another whip of squall cuts
pleasantries, they head back.

We turn from the shore.
Our reward glows.
Between sea and clouds
vermilion.

Philton

Looking at Oliver's Hill in Autumn

From a balcony over the dunes, the sea
in an impersonation of a lake, lies placid.
A quiescent watery giant, knowing he can rise
up anytime, exert his power, trample
the minions, make them quake.
He keeps his underlings, the fish in check.
Only a rebel few dare to leap up, make ripples.
Mist's elongated shadow adds an extra dimension.

Oliver's Hill becomes a saltwater croc;
jaws clamped shut. Houses are barnacles
on its back, the road a slithery scar.
Lazily, the crocodile shivers.
Stretches headfirst into
a cold sea of vaporised ether.

Avril Bradley

The Pyramids

Of course most people come here to see the pyramids, but we
  also have the leaning tower, the great wall and
  the grand canyon, our stump is blacker than all
  the others, our Bunnings was once the largest in
  the world, and the twin glaciers on Liddesdale
  Grove are almost a secret, but my personal
  favourite is the great salt basin that stretches
  halfway to the beginning of time,
  shimmering and whispering, shimmering and
  whispering.

Garth Madsen

Tardis

Outside
 squat and
  severe against the sky,
   you need to know it's there
   and everything it promises –
 a box of astronomical delights.
   Come through the door into the foyer
    where the witchery begins, welcome
     from a Dame resplendent in bronze.
      Come deeper, into the inner circle,
       and prepare to be enchanted,
        transported to other magical worlds.
         Here they all are: actors and acrobats,
          dancers and jugglers, operatic tenors,
          comedians, prima donnas of both sexes,
          soloists, ensembles, orchestras, choirs,
          understudies, stagehands, extras, stars.
         Come sit in the auditorium,
         drown in fizzing joy; the pure
         effervescence of live performance,
      all the entrances entrancing,
      and all the exits exciting.
    A building full of surprises. Who
     would think it could be so much
      bigger on the
 inside.

Mary Jones

City of Stars

In 1945 they constructed a city
fibro and weatherboard.
Sailed shiploads of Brits
into their dream homes –
a new world
crowded with meat pies
hamburgers and footy.
The newcomers shed overcoats
and let the southern sun
turn them brown.

Up the hill as you leave Centrelink
you lift your shoulder eastward
away from the bureaucrats,
jay walk to fresh scones jam and cream
midweek matinée of *Oklahoma*
Pretty palaces line the beachfront
the south is puffed with affluence,
along the wide avenues wattle blossom
showers pollen-thick light on the privileged.

The transformation happens quietly,
the library blooms – maybe a single derro
catching a nap in front of *Vogue* and *Delicious*
a coffee cart dispenses organic caffeine – soo us.
The ugly duckling abandons her skirts
for designer jeans and lycra
on the weekends.
Though you can't love me back I remain
Yours Faithfully.

Gwen McCallum

The end of the world

Ealing a childhood memory, the R100 his love
and failure, 'Airspeed'
his creation.
His slide-rule forsaken
for a pen and
A Town like Alice.

The nuclear holocaust for a time sparing our hemisphere.
Gardner and Peck in a film
about the end   of the world.

His 'Ambassador' in disguise, destroyed
by Munich ice.
In Manchester, that day, I cried
when Busby's Babes were killed
and Duncan Edwards lingered on.

The designer close to death himself
On the Beach   in Frankston

John Bradley

Contributors

Nan McClelland (1879–1961), poet and philanthropist, lived in Palm Court, Frankston, where in 1954 she and her brother established the first Peninsula Arts Society. Nan bequeathed money and land for the establishment of The McClelland Gallery and Sculpture Park.

Garth Madsen is the man who put the angst back into Frankston. He has been the self-appointed poet laureate for the city since he arrived in 1994.

Jennifer Compton lives in Melbourne, in Carrum, which is on the Frankston line. Five Islands Press recently released her book of poetry *Now You Shall Know*.

Warrick Wynne is a poet and teacher who, from his days at Frankston High, has had a lifelong love of the Mornington Peninsula. His latest book is *The State of the Rivers and Streams* (Five Islands Press).

Ann Simic was a Canberra academic who has relocated to Frankston via a circuitous route. Here she is involved in community radio, counselling, coaching, social justice and environmental issues.

Anne Elvey is the author of *Kin* (Five Islands Press, 2014) and editor of *Plumwood Mountain* journal. She lives in the Frankston municipality of Seaford, not far from the lovely but stressed Kananook Creek.

Glenn Harper lives in Frankston, is a lactose-intolerant teetotal vegetarian Gemini who does not believe in god, souls or astrology, and pretends to be a librarian.

Rhonda Jankovic (1963–2012), poet and social justice advocate, lived in Seaford. She inaugurated *Spoken Word* (3CR) 2009, giving a voice to many poets. *Your Heartbeat in Mine* (Pulse, 2012) was published posthumously. A poetry prize was established in her honour (2013).

Michael Potter is a Mornington Peninsula-based poet who has many soft spots for Frankston. Michael received some of his formal education and much of his informal education in the City by the Bay.

Gwen McCallum lived in Frankston from 1990 to 2012. She co-wrote a book of poetry, *Word Generation*, with A. Griffiths. Her latest collection is *The Hole in Lola's Tights* (MPU, 2012).

Mal Morgan, born in London in 1935, became the patriarch of Melbourne poetry at the end of last century. He published seven collections of his own poetry and was a major force behind the La Mama Poetica readings and the Montsalvat National Poetry Festivals in Eltham. He moved to Seaford and died there too young in 1999.

Marjorie Darling Ward has lived in Frankston for thirty years. She has published five books, a stage play and some poetry. She will not move unless the beach, the bay and the view from Oliver's Hill come too.

Philton has published poetry in national and international magazines. His poetry/fiction has won twenty-one first prizes. He has performed on ABC's *Poetica*. Oliver's Hill is named after his great great grandfather, John Oliver.

Avril Bradley fell in love with Oliver's Hill in 1971 when she arrived as a £10 Pom. She has lived in Frankston since 1999. Her latest poetry collection is *The Fragile Geometry of Dancers* (Ginninderra Press Pocket Poets).

Mary Jones is a writer and performance poet living in Mornington. She's an incorrigible theatre fanatic and often to be found hanging around Frankston Arts Centre. She blogs at maryjonesthewriter.com

John Bradley was an engineer and businessman. For thirty years he employed a secretary. On retirement he was promoted and is now his wife's secretary.

Acknowledgements

Avril Bradley: 'Down Oliver's' appeared in *Once upon a Sonnet* (Melbourne Shakespeare Society 2014); 'An English Immigrant's Letter' appeared in *Paradise Anthology,* no. 7, 2014; 'Looking at Oliver's Hill in Autumn' appeared in a special edition of *The Mozzie*, 'Poems About Place', 2015.

Jennifer Compton: 'The Frankston Massage' appeared in *Quadrant*, vol. 58, 1–2, 2014, and in *Best Australian Poems 2014*; 'The Raspberry Coloured Hand Knitted Cardigan' appeared in *Island*, 126.

Anne Elvey: 'Bayside Suburban' appeared in *Australian Book Review* 339, 2012, and in *Kin*, Five Islands Press, 2014.

Rhonda Jankovic: ''An Urbane Affair' appeared in *Positive Words*, 2011, and *The Mozzie*, 2011; 'Safe Haven' appeared in her posthumous collection *Your Heartbeat in Mine*, Pulse Publications, 2012. Both poems are used with permission of the publisher.

Garth Madsen: 'Frankston Train' appeared in *Blue Dog*, vol. 7, 2008; 'Superwomen' appeared in *Adventure Holiday*, Wagtail 92, Picaro Press, 2009.

Gwen McCallum: 'Frankston Station' appeared in *Word Generation*.

Nan McClelland: 'The Fairies and I' appeared in *The Poems and Works of Miss Nan McClelland*, c. 1990. The poem is used with permission of the publisher, The Trustees of the Estate of A.M. McClelland.

Mal Morgan: 'Afghan Restaurant' appeared in *Beautiful Veins*, Five Islands Press, 1999. The poem is used with permission of the publisher.

Mick Potter: 'The Fine Art of Surfacing' appeared in *Pearl Magazine*, issue 22, 2013.

Warrick Wynne: 'Beginnings' and 'The day it snowed in Frankston' appeared in *The State of the Rivers and Streams*, Five Islands Press; 'Beginnings' (formerly 'The Street of the Dead') also appeared in *Quadrant*.

www.ingramcontent.com/pod-product-compliance
Lightning Source LLC
Chambersburg PA
CBHW062203100526
44589CB00014B/1931